Animals I See at the Zoo

SNAKES

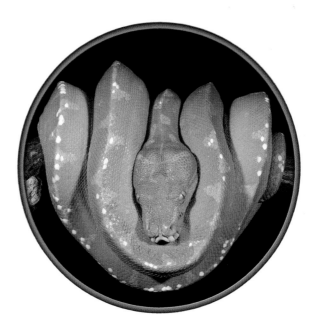

by JoAnn Early Macken

Reading consultant: Susan Nations, M.Ed., author/literacy coach/consultant

WEEKLY WR READER®
EARLY LEARNING LIBRARY

Please visit our web site at: **www.earlyliteracy.cc**
For a free color catalog describing Weekly Reader® Early Learning Library's
list of high-quality books, call 1-877-445-5824 (USA) or 1-800-387-3178 (Canada).
Weekly Reader® Early Learning Library's fax: (414) 336-0164.

Library of Congress Cataloging-in-Publication Data

Macken, JoAnn Early, 1953-
    Snakes / by JoAnn Early Macken.
      p. cm. — (Animals I see at the zoo)
    Summary: A simple introduction to snakes and some of their characteristics.
    Includes bibliographical references and index.
    ISBN 0-8368-3275-2 (lib. bdg.)
    ISBN 0-8368-3288-4 (softcover)
    1. Snakes—Juvenile literature. 2. Zoo animals—Juvenile literature. [1. Snakes.
  2. Zoo animals.] I. Title.
QL666.O6M194   2002
597.96—dc21   2002016863

This edition first published in 2002 by
Weekly Reader® Early Learning Library
330 West Olive Street, Suite 100
Milwaukee, WI 53212 USA

Art direction: Tammy Gruenewald
Production: Susan Ashley
Photo research: Diane Laska-Swanke
Graphic design: Katherine A. Goedheer

Photo credits: Cover, title, pp. 17, 21 © James P. Rowan; p. 5 © William Muñoz; p. 7 © Richard
Thom/Visuals Unlimited; p. 9 © Jim Merli/Visuals Unlimited; p. 11 © Joel Arrington/Visuals
Unlimited; p. 13 © Bayard Brattstrom/Visuals Unlimited; p. 15 © Gilbert Twiest/Visuals Unlimited;
p. 19 © Bill Draker/KAC Productions

Printed in the United States of America

1 2 3 4 5 6 7 8 9 06 05 04 03 02

Note to Educators and Parents

Reading is such an exciting adventure for young children! They are beginning to integrate their oral language skills with written language. To encourage children along the path to early literacy, books must be colorful, engaging, and interesting; they should invite the young reader to explore both the print and the pictures.

Animals I See at the Zoo is a new series designed to help children read about twelve fascinating animals. In each book, young readers will learn interesting facts about the featured animal.

Each book is specially designed to support the young reader in the reading process. The familiar topics are appealing to young children and invite them to read — and re-read — again and again. The full-color photographs and enhanced text further support the student during the reading process.

In addition to serving as wonderful picture books in schools, libraries, homes, and other places where children learn to love reading, these books are specifically intended to be read within an instructional guided reading group. This small group setting allows beginning readers to work with a fluent adult model as they make meaning from the text. After children develop fluency with the text and content, the book can be read independently. Children and adults alike will find these books supportive, engaging, and fun!

— Susan Nations, M.Ed., author, literacy coach,
and consultant in literacy development

I like to go to the zoo. I see snakes at the zoo.

Some snakes climb trees. Green snakes can hide in the leaves.

Some snakes live under the ground. They dig nests under the ground.

Some snakes swim in water. They move from side to side as they swim.

Some snakes live in the desert. They leave trails as they glide in the sand.

Some snakes
have marks to
help them hide.
Can you see the
snake in this
picture?

Snakes smell with their tongues. They find food with their tongues.

Snakes do not hear well. They know that danger is near when they feel the ground shake.

I like to see
snakes at the
zoo. Do you?

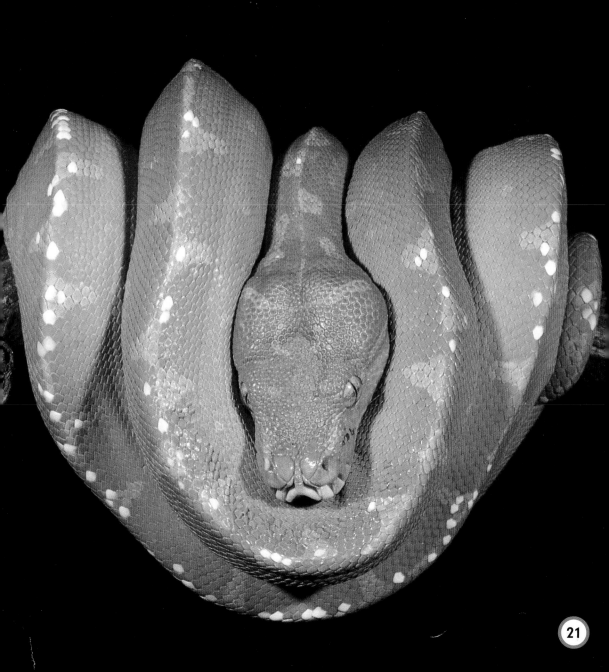

Glossary

danger — something that may cause harm

desert — dry land with few plants

glide — to move smoothly and easily

trails — marks left by a moving body

For More Information

Books

Ling, Mary, and Mary Atkinson. *The Snake Book.*
    New York: Dorling Kindersley, 2000.
Macken, JoAnn Early. *Rain Forest Animals. Animal Worlds*
    (series). Milwaukee: Gareth Stevens, 2002.
Patent, Dorothy Hinshaw. *Slinky Scaly Slithery Snakes.*
    New York: Walker and Co., 2000.
Simon, Seymour. *Snakes.* New York: HarperCollins, 1992.

Web Sites

Lincoln Park Zoo

zoo.interaccess.com/tour/factsheets/herps/ball_python.html
For a ball python photo and facts
zoo.interaccess.com/tour/factsheets/herps/g_t_python.html
For a green tree python photo and facts

Woodland Park Zoo

www.zoo.org/educate/fact_sheets/day/boa_c.htm
For a boa constrictor photo, map, and facts

Index

About the Author

JoAnn Early Macken is the author of a rhyming picture book, *Cats on Judy*, and *Animal Worlds*, a series of nonfiction picture books about animals and their habitats. Her poems have been published or accepted by *Ladybug*, *Spider*, *Highlights for Children*, and an anthology, *Stories from Where We Live: The Great Lakes*. A winner of the Barbara Juster Esbensen 2000 Poetry Teaching Award, she teaches poetry writing. She lives in Wisconsin with her husband and their two sons.